The Fruit of the Spirit

A journey where conviction and
encouragement intersect

THROUGH THE WORD

Flourish Through the Word is a community of women of all ages who gather weekly to worship, pray, study the Bible together, and build relationships. From these weekly gatherings, women are then equipped to move out into their arenas of influence and be a light for Jesus.

Flourish is a 501C3 ministry that is supported by the material fees charged for the studies and private donations. If you'd like to find out more about the ministry or make a tax-deductible donation, please visit _flourishthroughtheword.com_.

Donations can be made online or by mailing a check to:

Flourish Through the Word
2020 Maltby Rd, PMB 240
Bothell WA 98021

On our website are various Bible study teaching sessions based on the studies our community has done together. These are easily viewed for use in home, church, or small group. Please contact our ministry for more details.

ISBN: 979-8-9909136-1-5

A word about fruit

There is quite a contrast between works and fruit. A machine in a factory works and turns out a product, but it could never manufacture fruit.

Fruit grows out of life, and for the believer in Jesus, it is the life of the Spirit.

When you think of 'works,' you think of effort, labor, strain, and toil; when you think of 'fruit' you think of beauty, quietness, sweetness, the unfolding of a life.

The Holy Spirit produces living fruit and this fruit has in it the seed for still more fruit. Jesus is concerned that we produce fruit...more fruit...and much fruit (see John 15), because this is the way we glorify Him.

The fruit of the Spirit in this six-week study reveals character that is produced from God as we yield our lives to Him.

The New Testament writers emphasized different aspects of the Hoy Spirit's work. John highlighted the Spirit's role as teacher. In Acts, Luke focused on the Spirit's guidance and power for evangelism, and the importance of being filled with the Spirit.

Paul provides us with a comprehensive view of the Spirit's work. This study is just a little slice of that!

The Holy Spirit brings new life in Christ, gives Christians power over sin, power for ministry, and power to live a fruitful life.

May this study of the nine fruits or character qualities of God, deemed the 'fruits of the Spirit,' cause you to hunger for more of Him and the Holy Spirit's work in your life.

Be sure to read all of the commentary written with each question as each week is designed for you to go deeper into the Word of God as you give yourself to the study of the fruit of the Spirit.

May Jesus be glorified and lifted up in your life,

May this study of the fruit of the Spirit draw your heart even closer to God as you learn more about His unchanging character and love for you.

My prayer is for the Lord to use this study powerfully in your life!

Week One

Establishing our foundation

Our journey in this study of the fruit of the Spirit starts with us diving into the book of Galatians. We start here to gain the context of Paul's listing of the nine fruits. We will be unpacking the fifth chapter of this amazing letter to the believers living in Galatia, as this will provide us with a firm foundation for our study.

The Galatian church were sticklers for the right thing done the right way and in the right order. Paul addressed this in his letter to them. It would be very helpful for you to take the time to **read the entire lette**r to get the full context of Paul's message to them

May God bless you as you begin and may He open even more of your heart to His wonderful Word!

1. Read the entire book (letter) of Galatians and write out one salient point from each chapter you read:

    *   Galatians 1:

    *   Galatians 2:

    *   Galatians 3:

    *   Galatians 4:

    *   Galatians 5:

    *   Galatians 6:

LOVE JOY PEACE PATIENCE KINDNESS GOODNESS FAITHFULNESS GENTLENESS SELF-CONTROL

2. What are you specifically asking the Lord to do in your life through this this study of the fruit of the Spirit? Write out your prayer here and commit yourself fully to Him as you begin.

Today we turn our attention to Galatians 5. Many people in the first century declared that Paul's doctrine of grace was dangerous because they felt it replaced law with license. They believed if rules and high standards were abandoned, the churches would fall apart.

Have you seen these same attitudes today?

Legalists in our churches and Christian culture today warn that we dare not teach people about the liberty and freedom we have in Christ because it could lead to religious anarchy.

Paul used his divinely inspired letter to teach the church how to apply the practical aspects of living by faith and walking in grace.

Paul desired us to experience the *inner* discipline of our relationship with God, teaching us that through Him and His precious Holy Spirit, we would be equipped to walk and live in faith. This divine enablement would far outweigh any man-made rules and laws. The Christian who depends on the power of the Spirit by yielding to God and His grace, will not be rebelling against the law of God, but rather Scripture shows us that God's law is being fulfilled in us as we live by the Spirit.

1. Before you read Galatians 5, look up Romans 8:1-4 and list out the facts from this passage.

2. Read Galatians 5:1-12. What title would you give this section of Scripture? Explain why in the space below.

3. Write out Galatians 5:1 here.

4. The freedom Paul wrote about is the deliverance from the curse that the law pronounces on sinners who have been striving to achieve their own righteousness. What do you learn about this freedom from the following passages.

- Galatians 3:13

- Galatians 3:22-26

- Galatians 4:1-7

5. What is the one thing that guarantees our freedom in Christ?

In this letter to the church in Galatia, we see how the legalists claim the answer to problems was in existing laws. Paul explained how no amount of legislation could change people's hearts. It is not the law on the outside but love on the inside that makes the difference.

We all need a power within us to change our hearts and lives. That power comes from the Holy Spirit.

Read Galatians 5:13-26 before you begin your study today.

1. There are at least fourteen references to the Holy Spirit in Galatians. Look up these three and write out what you glean from each one:

    •   Galatians 3:2

    •   Galatians 4:6

    •   Galatians 4:29

2. The Holy Spirit is a divine Person. What God the Father **planned** for you, and God the Son **purchased** for you on the cross, God the Spirit **personalizes** for you and applies it to your life as you yield to Him. This final section of Chapter 5 is one of the most crucial parts of Scripture because here Paul explains the three ministries of the Holy Spirit. Read Galatians 5:13-15. Explain our calling as Christians and what we are free from.

3. After explaining our call, Paul then issues a warning to us. Write it out here.

4. One of the three ministries of the Holy Spirit is He **enables us to fulfill the law of love**. The Holy Spirit within gives us the love that we need. Look up the following verses and tell how the Holy Spirit enables us.

    *   Romans 5:5

    *   Galatians 5:6

    *   Galatians 5:22

> "The Holy Spirit does not work in a vacuum. He uses the Word of God, prayer, worship, and the fellowship of believers to build us up in Christ. The believer who spends time daily in the Word and prayer, and who yields to the Spirit's working, is going to enjoy freedom and will help build up the church."
> ~Warren Wiersbe

The second way the Holy Spirit enables us to enjoy freedom in Christ is by **helping us to overcome the flesh**. What did Paul mean by 'the flesh?' He was not talking about the body, as the human body is neutral. Paul wanted us to know that when we walk in the Spirit and allow Him to control us, we will not be driven by our fleshly desires and appetites. The Holy Spirit and the 'flesh' have opposite appetites, and this is what causes the conflict. Let's dig in today to find out more about the Holy Spirit's power in this area.

1. Read Galatians 5:16-21 and 24 today. Write out the conflict as stated in verses 16-17.

2. Write out the message these additional verses express about the conflict in Romans 7:15 and 19.

3. Paul pointed out that we cannot win this victory in our strength and by our own willpower. The solution is to surrender our will to the Holy Spirit. Write out the key from Galatians 5:18.

4. For further encouragement from the Holy Spirit, read Hebrews 10:14-17. Write out the truth from this passage and tell how we are equipped to be victorious.

5. Read Galatians 5:19-21 and 24 to answer the questions. Paul lists some of the sins that characterize mankind living under the law. His list encompasses three areas of human life: sex, religion, and relationships. Write out what Paul says is the benefit of those who belong to Christ in verse 24. What is the practical outworking of this verse in the battle of the flesh vs. the Spirit?

6. What encouragement do you receive from Romans 8:12-14?

"Christ not only died for me, but I died with Christ. Christ died for me to remove the penalty of my sin, but I died with Christ to break sin's power." ~Warren Wiersbe

We have seen from our brief study in Galatians 5 how the Spirit enables us to fulfill the law of love, to overcome the flesh, and now we will see today how **the Spirit enables us to produce fruit**.

The Holy Spirit produces living fruit and this fruit has in it the seed for more fruit. Jesus told his followers in John 15:2 and 5:

> *"He cuts off every branch of mine that doesn't produce fruit, and he prunes the branches that do bear fruit so they will produce even more. Yes, I am the vine; you are the branches. Those who remain in me, and I in them, will produce much fruit. For apart from me you can do nothing."*

Bearing fruit is how we glorify Jesus! The old nature cannot produce fruit; only the new nature can do that.

Read Galatians 5:22-23 and 25-26 to answer the questions for today.

1. The fruit of the Spirit listed in this passage has to do with character. List out the fruit here:

2. When a Christian walks by the Spirit and manifests fruit, this believer does not need an external law to produce the attitudes and behavior that please God. What do you learn from Romans 8:4 about this?

3. In Galatians 5:25-26, Paul instructs us on how there needs to be a right atmosphere in order for the fruit to grow. Tell practically how we 'keep in step with the Spirit'. Which aspects of a right atmosphere would aid in cultivating the fruit of the Spirit?

4. Summarize in two or three points what you have learned from this week's study of Galatians.

Week Two

The fruit of the Spirit is Love

> ***"...the fruit of the Spirit is love, joy, peace, patience, kindness, goodness, faithfulness, gentleness, self-control; against such things there is no law"*** (Galatians 5:22-23).

What initially comes to mind when you think of the fruit of the Spirit? Do you conjure up a list of legalistic behaviors? Do you begin to grade yourself based on this list in Galatians? What is so important about these nine things anyway?

As we dig into this list of nine godly characteristics, we will see that these are the things the Lord desires to be present in our lives. These attributes truly describe Him, and as we get to know the Lord better, the fruit produced in our lives will be a by-product of our relationship with Jesus.

1. Please note in the verse above that the word *fruit* is singular. This is a collective list of fruits and is reflective of our connection to the Holy Spirit. Paul, as he wrote this letter, used the word fruit to describe the wonderful things the Holy Spirit wants to produce inside our lives. Write out why you think Paul chose fruit to describe this list of godly qualities. As you do this, answer this question with your favorite fruit in mind.

2. Paul had previously described the works of the flesh in Galatians 5:19-21. You studied this last week, but read the passage again and describe the contrast between the flesh and the Spirit.

---

3. Al fruit is produced from some kind of seed. Read Genesis 1:11-12. Write out what you learn from this passage. How does the kind of seed sown determine the fruit produced?

4. Read 1 Peter 1:23 and write out the truth of this Scripture here.

5. The moment you received Jesus as your Savior by faith, God sowed His Spirit and His Word into your heart like a seed. His Word is incorruptible. If His Word and His Spirit have been sown into your heart like a seed, what kind of fruit can you expect from Him? As you answer this question, which steps do you need to take for the Holy Spirit to produce more fruit in your life? For example, what role will your commitment to this Bible study or prayer play in your life as you draw closer to Him?

6. Faul begins his list with love because all of the other fruit is really an outgrowth of love. The Greek word used here is *agape.* In the New Testament, the best example of *agape* is found in John 3:16. Write out the verse here and explain why it depicts the best example of love.

Today we continue our study of the fruit of **agape** or love.

> *"Agape is so filled with deep emotion and meaning that it is one of the most difficult words to translate in the New Testament. Agape occurs when an individual sees, recognizes, understands, or appreciates the value of an object or a person, causing the viewer to behold this object or person in great esteem, awe, admiration, wonder, and sincere appreciation. Such great respect is awakened in the heart of the observer for the object or person he is beholding that he is compelled to love it. In fact, his love for that person or object is so strong that it is irresistible.*
>
> *Agape is a love that that loves so profoundly that it knows no limits or boundaries in how far, wide, high, and deep it will go to show that love to its recipient. Agape is the highest form of love—a self-sacrificial type of love that moves the lover to action."* (Renner, Sparkling Gems from the Greek, page 525)

1. Compare the eight qualities of the fruit that flow from love in Galatians 5:22-23 with the characteristics of love given in 1 Corinthians 13:4-8.

2. Can you think of a person in your life who has or does love you with agape love? What kind of impact did that love have on you? Read 1 Corinthians 13, the love chapter, out loud. Pray over what you have read and ask the Lord to supernaturally cause His love to flow through you so that you can love others this way.

3. Write out 1 John 3:16 and explain what this means in having agape love for each other.

4. Agape is a love that has no strings attached. This kind of divine love isn't looking for what it can get, but for what it can give. Because the seed of God's Word is sown into your heart, and the Holy Spirit lives inside you, the potential for this love is within you. Is the Holy Spirit prompting you through your study so far to set aside anything that could be hindering you from this kind of agape love? Write out your prayer to Him here.

We are learning that *agape* love is the source fruit of the Spirit from where all other fruits are an outgrowth. Love is relational.

1. Read 1 John 4:7-8. Write the facts of this passage from your reading.

2. Verse 7 in the passage above is the key to this passage. What can you actively do to make sure that love is your habitual practice?

3. How does this passage define God?

4. In any community, be it family, church, work, or anywhere, the inevitable conflict will arise. Galatians 5:16, 22-23, 25-26 gives us specific and practical ways we can navigate through conflict. Write out each practical step here.

5. How do the steps you recorded above keep you in alignment with the Father, Son, and Holy Spirit? How do these steps reflect *agape* love?

The last two days of this week's study have us taking a realistic look into our own hearts when it comes to relationships. As said in yesterday's homework, no matter where we live or whatever season we are currently in, we can count on misunderstanding, disappointment, or conflict with other people as a part of our existence.

This being true, how do we apply the practical outworking of *agape* love in our relationships? How do we keep in step with the Spirit when it comes to our interaction with others? Prayerfully approach these last two days, keeping in mind the fruit of the Spirit of love.

1 Corinthians 13:5 tells us, ***"Love is not irritable or touchy. It does not hold grudges and will hardly even notice when others do it wrong."***

1. Spend some time praying through the verse above and memorize it. Write it on an index card and keep it with you to review. This is one practical way of keeping in step with the Spirit.

2. Look up the Scriptures that go with each item and write how the verse applies to each one as we deal with conflict in relationships while seeking to keep in step with the Spirit and ***agape*-**love others:

    • Ask God to rewire your soul. 1 Corinthians 13:5:

    • Ask the Holy Spirit to reveal unresolved issues. Psalm 139:23-24:

    • Choose not to remember the sins committed against you. Hebrews 8:12:

- Refuse to be defensive. Proverbs 27:6:

- Decide to always believe the best about people. 1 Corinthians 13:7:

- Memorize related Scripture. James 1:19:

- Pray blessings over your enemies. 1 Peter 3:9:

Because of Jesus, it is possible for you and me to have right relationships with God, with each other within our homes, within our churches and with relationships we thought could never be repaired.
~Nancy Demoss Wolgemuth

We wrap up this week by taking a look at some of the 'one anothers' in Scripture. The Lord has given us His wisdom on how to be together, how to treat one another, and how to love one another.

1. Look up each verse and write the commands given in each.

    - Galatians 5:13-14

    - Galatians 6:2

    - Hebrews 3:13

    - 2 Corinthians 13:11

    - Hebrews 10:24

    - Ephesians 4:32

2. Look up each verse and write what you learn about interaction in your relationships.

    •   Ephesians 5:21

    •   Romans 15:7

    •   1 Thessalonians 5:13

3. Summarize how the Lord has spoken to you through your study of His Word this week. Write your thoughts in the form of a prayer to Him.

Week Three

The fruit of the Spirit is Joy

The character that God wants in our lives is seen in the nine 'fruits' of the Spirit. Last week we learned how Paul began with love because all the other fruit is really an outgrowth of love.

When a person lives in the sphere of love, then joy is a natural experience.

What is joy? It can be simply defined as *inner quiet peace and well-being that is not affected by outward circumstances but is a result of being with Jesus.*

The Greek word for joy is **chara**, derived from the word **charis**, which is Greek for grace. This is significant for us because it reveals that joy is produced by the grace of God.

This means joy is not human-based happiness that ebbs and flows. Joy is truly divine in its origin, a fruit of the Spirit that gives expression and flourishes best when times are hard.

1. Before we get started, take a few minutes to prayerfully reflect on the current status of your joy. How is your joy level? Have you recently experienced something difficult in your life, but remained joyful throughout? What are you grateful for? Write your answers in the space below, asking the Lord to reveal new things out of His Word to you through this study.

2. Look up Nehemiah 8:10. Write the verse out here and explain what it means to you to have this type of joy.

3. In the Old Testament verse above, the people were encouraged to rejoice. They had a reason to celebrate. Read aloud Psalm 100 and list out the facts from this psalm here. Spend time praising the Lord for His goodness, love, and faithfulness.

4. Your personal challenge for today and each day throughout this study is outlined for you in this simple J-O-Y acrostic. Take the time today to purposefully engage with the three aspects provided here. You will be revisiting this throughout the rest of the study.

J—Jesus
Set aside time each day to praise the Lord, thanking Him for Who He is, for all He gives, and for all He does in your life. Set your timer and tell Him out loud what you are grateful for and why you are praising Him. Write down three specific things a day that you are thankful for. As you continually worship and praise Jesus, you will discover more of His Presence in your daily life. Make praise and thanks your default.

O—Others
Praying for others is one of the greatest investments we can ever make. Take time each day to pray for the needs and concerns of others in your life.

- Your family and loved ones.
- Your city, our nation, and your region.
- Local schools in your neighborhood.
- Your church, Bible study, and Christian community "...that the Word of the Lord may be spread rapidly and be honored." (2 Thessalonians 3:1)
- Renewed passion for evangelism.
- More power from the Holy Spirit.
- Unity in our churches.

Y—You
The Lord has called us to go and make disciples. We won't be able to do this unless we are taking the time to be equipped through His Word. Ask the Lord to give you a hunger for His Word and a hunger for righteousness, along with a desire to fellowship with Him each day. Prayerfully focus on the following as you seek to pursue Him.

- Use the Bible each day to become more connected to God.
- Listen to the Lord as you read His Word, cultivate a listening ear for whatever He wants to speak to you.
- Be willing to go out of your way to encourage and build up others.
- Rejoice about the future.
- Believe the promises of God.
- Keep your eyes on Jesus, the Author and Finisher of our faith.

Love Joy Peace Patience Kindness Goodness Faithfulness Gentleness Self-control

Despite his difficult circumstances as a prisoner in Rome, Paul rejoiced. The secret to his joy was in the fact that he lived for Christ and the gospel. While in prison, Paul penned another letter to his friends who had formed the church in Phillipi. This letter to the Philippians is known as the joy book.

By way of review, here's our simple definition of joy: *inner quiet peace and well-being that is not affected by outward circumstances but is a result of being with Jesus.*

We will spend the next two days exploring the truth of what Paul discovered by visiting his letter to the Philippians as we learn more about joy.

Read all of Philippians 2 today.

1. Write out the facts from Philippians 2:1-4. What specifically jumped out to you as you wrote down each fact?

2. According to verse one, how do we receive encouragement from Christ? How does this parallel what we are learning about the fruit of the Spirit?

3. What did Paul mean by 'completing his joy' in verse 2?

4. In verse 3, Paul directly addresses selfish ambition which can cause strife, rivalry, or partisanship. This is the person who is concerned only with her own welfare. How does selfishness impact our joy?

5. In verses 3-4 Paul provides us with practical ways of combatting selfish ambition and conceit. List those here and turn your answer into a personal prayer.

We are focusing on the fruit of the Spirit of joy this week.

Before you begin today's lesson, go back to the JOY page on day one and pray through the points provided for you.

Read Philippians 2:5-11 for today and read it over several times and in several translations. This passage has been historically described as the most sublime passage of the whole New Testament.

1. Why do you think this passage is so sublime? How does it relate to joy?

2. Jesus is the ultimate example of selfless humility. Write out everything this passage tells us about the specific things Jesus did and how He lived.

3. Having the 'mind' of Christ (verse 5) means having the attitude of Christ. Why is this so important and how does this impact the fruit of the Spirit of joy?

4. What can you specifically practice in your life to cultivate more of the attitude of Christ?

"The longer I live, the more I realize the impact of attitude on life. Attitude to me is more important than facts. It is more important than the past, than education, than money, than circumstances, than failures, than successes, than what other people think or say or do. It is more important than appearance, giftedness or skill. It will make or break a company, a school, or a home. The remarkable thing is we have a choice every day regarding the attitude we will embrace for that day. We cannot change our past; we cannot change the fact that people will act in a certain way. We cannot change the inevitable. The only thing we can do is plan on the one thing we have, and that is our attitude. I am convinced that life is 10% what happens to me and 90% how I react to it." —Pastor and author, Chuck Swindoll

The blessed hope of Christ's return and our eternal life with Him, casts its gracious influence and joy over all of life. Paul prayed that believers will have joy at all times and not be worried or anxious.

Read all of Philippians 4 today.

1. What command was given to us in Philippians 4:4?

2. Why are we to rejoice always? Use Romans 12:12 to help you answer.

3. Paul also wrote another letter and issued a similar command. Read 1 Thessalonians 5:16-19 and list out all of the practical ways we can cultivate the fruit of rejoicing always.

4. How do we quench the Holy Spirit? Read Ephesians 4:29-31 to help you answer.

5. How can a Christian rejoice, even in the midst of extremely difficult or even tragic circumstances? Use the following Scriptures to help you answer:

- Philippians 4:12

- Habakkuk 3:17-18

- 2 Corinthians 6:4-10

- 1 Peter 4:12-13

We have spent this week exploring the truth of joy throughout several Bible passages, with a focus being on Paul's encouraging letter about joy that he penned while in prison.

Today will be an exercise in practicing what you have learned so far. We could spend the rest of our lives learning about the spiritual fruit of joy as we intentionally practice rejoicing each day.

Read the attached article and then take the time to declare the verses on praise provided on the next few pages.

Plan to revisit the praise declarations as well as the JOY acrostic from day one.

Why we need to praise God more

– Stormie Omartian

Worshiping God is not just about singing praise songs in church once a week. Worship and praise is what we do in the car on the way to work, to school, or to the store. It's what we have in our heart when we're in the mall, the airport, or the doctor's office.

It is what we do when the kitchen sink stops up, the car has a flat tire, we become sick, or we've lost our keys for the millionth time. It's what we speak fervently when we are in the emergency room, at a loved one's burial, or in the middle of the storm. It's an ongoing attitude of the heart. An attitude that doesn't change, no matter what else in your life does.

I'm not talking about some kind of positive thinking. This is not a plunge into denial. I'm talking about looking at the reality of your life straight on and declaring an even greater reality straight over it. Instead of letting yourself sink to the level of the problem, make yourself rise to the level of the solution.

One of the secrets of experiencing the power of praise is to make a decision that you will worship God no matter what your circumstances are. When you get to the place where praise comes automatically, no matter what is going on, you will come to know God more intimately. And when you do, you won't be able to stop yourself from praising Him.

When we make our first reaction to what happens in our lives, a reaffirming praise to God for who He is, we invite His presence to inhabit the situation and His power to come and change things. This is the hidden power of praising God.

God wants you to exalt Him and not your problems. The more you praise Him, the more you are centered on Him, and the more you will be relieved of the burden of those problems. This doesn't mean you are pretending they do not exist. It means you are saying, "Although I have these problems, I know that You, Lord, are greater than they are. You created me. You are my heavenly Father; You are a good God. In You is everything I need for my life, and I choose to exalt You above all."

When you become convinced of the power of praise in every situation, and understand all that is accomplished when you are a true worshiper of God, your life will be changed forever.

Praise Declarations from Scripture

"I will bless the Lord at all times; His praise shall continually be in my mouth.
My soul shall make its boast in the Lord; the humble shall hear of it and be glad.
Oh, magnify the Lord with me, and let us exalt His name together" (Psalm 34:1-3).

"I will sing to the Lord for He has triumphed gloriously! The Lord is my strength and my song,
and He has become my salvation; He is my God and I will praise Him" (Exodus 15:1-2).

"The boundary lines have fallen for me in pleasant places" (Psalm 16:5).

"I will sing to the Lord for He has been good to me" (Psalm 13:6).

"Gracious is the Lord and righteous; yes, our God is merciful" (Psalm 117:2).

"Praise the Lord! Praise the Lord, O my soul! While I live will I praise the Lord. I will sing praises
to my God while I have my being. Happy is he who has the God of Jacob for his help,
whose hope is in the Lord his God" (Psalm 146:1-5).

"My lips shall utter praise, for You teach me Your statutes" (Psalm 119:171).

"How great is Your goodness which You have laid up for those who fear You,
which You have prepared for those who trust in You" (Psalm 31:19).

"For I proclaim the name of the Lord: Ascribe greatness to our God.
His is the Rock; His work is perfect; for all His ways are justice.
A God of truth and without injustice, righteous and upright is He" (Deuteronomy 32:3-4).

"Satisfy us in the morning with Your faithful love
so that we may shout with joy and be glad all our days" (Psalm 90:14).

"Let God arise and let His enemies be scattered; let those also who hate Him flee before Him.
But let the righteous be glad; let them rejoice before God; yes, let them rejoice exceedingly.
Sing to God, sing praises to His name" (Psalm 68:1, 3-4).

"I will give You thanks in the great assembly; I will praise You among many people" (Psalm 35:18).

Week Four

The fruit of the Spirit is Peace

We've been learning about the fruit of the Spirit and have so far studied love and joy. This week we will see what the Bible teaches about peace. Love and joy together produce peace.

The word peace comes from the Greek word *eirene*, which is the Greek equivalent of the Hebrew word **shalom.**

> *"Shalom expresses the idea of wholeness, completeness, or tranquility in the soul that is unaffected by outward circumstances or pressures. The word **eirene** strongly suggests the rule of order in place of chaos. When a person is dominated by peace, he has a calm, inner stability that results in the ability to conduct himself peacefully, even in the midst of circumstances that would normally be very nerve-racking, traumatic, or upsetting. Rather than allowing the difficulties and pressures of life to break him, a person who is possessed by **eirene** is whole, complete, orderly, stable, and poised for blessing."*
> ~Renner, Sparkling Gems from the Greek, page 529

The New Testament provides us with examples of supernatural peace that the Holy Spirit produces.

Read Acts 27:1-43.

1. This chapter tells the amazing story of Paul's journey on a ship that was dangerously tossed back and forth by the raging sea. List several aspects of how bad the storm was for Paul and everyone aboard the ship.

2. Acts 27:20 tells more of how serious the storm was. Write out this verse and think about how this description could be a metaphor for when things are seriously 'stormy' in our own lives. Include your insights here.

3. What did Paul say right in the midst of all this hopelessness in Acts 27:21-25?

4. Paul had heard from the Lord which caused supernatural peace to rise up within him. How did Paul's peace bring strength to the others on the ship? Review the definition of peace (*eirene*) given at the start of this lesson and record your insights of how Paul was calm and displayed inner stability even though the circumstances looked dire.

5. Applying what you learn from Paul in this account of the storm, write down how the Holy Spirit provides you with peace when difficult or challenging moments come your way. Can you think of a time when the peace of God replaced fear or worry in your life? How does the Holy Spirit release His dominating peace in your life in the face of hard circumstances? If you currently need more of His peace in your life right now, write your prayer here.

6. Take some time to review the praise declarations given in the homework of Week Three.

The salvation provided to us by Jesus is the reason we can experience peace. We are reconciled to God through the blood of the cross. He cleanses us of sin, and we can now look with confidence to God and to others.

1. Look up and write down the truth of Proverbs 16:7.

2. Look up the following Scriptures and write out what the Bible says about peace:

    • 2 Thessalonians 3:16

    • Colossians 3:15

    • Matthew 5:9

    • Isaiah 26:3

    • Psalm 4:8

3. Take time today to write out what the Lord is revealing to you from His Word about peace. Write out your thoughts in the form of a prayer here. Take some time to revisit the JOY steps from last week.

When we are rooted in Jesus, we are equipped to be in a consistent state of well-being. We've seen Paul's response when he was caught in a life-threatening storm. He knew his life was rooted in Jesus and no matter what happened on that boat, Paul knew his life was secure.

We learn much from Paul's writings and his life in the New Testament. Let's revisit what he had to say in his letter to his friends in Philippi.

Read Philippians 4:6-7.

1. Write out the facts and the direct commands in verse 6 of this passage.

2. Jesus had some things to say about anxiety. Read Matthew 6:25-33. List out in bullet points all the things Jesus emphasized to us about worry and concern.

3. Paul urged us to pray about the burdens of our hearts and minds in Philippians 4:6: *...in everything by prayer and supplication with thanksgiving let your requests be made known to God.* When seeking to grow in our relationship with Jesus and to then naturally bear the fruit of the Holy Spirit, these three types of prayer are extremely practical.

   PRAYER: Look up each Scripture and write the truth of prayer that you glean from each:

   - Matthew 6:7-8

   - Matthew 7:1-11

   - Hebrews 5:7

   SUPPLICATION: this is praying with earnest intensity. Write what you learn from these verses:

   - Romans 15:30

   - Colossians 4:12

   THANKSGIVING: What do you learn from these verses?

   - Ephesians 5:20

   - Colossians 3:15-17

   - Luke 17:11-19

4. In Philippians 4:7, what did Paul say would be the fruit of our prayers? Wrap up today's study with some prayer time of your own.

Our focus this week has been on the fruit of the Spirit, peace.

Jesus taught us about peace as well and had much to say about it.

1. Read John 14:27 and write out the verse here.

2. Is this type of '**shalom**' peace that Jesus spoke of in this verse available to those people who do not have a saving relationship with Him? Why or why not?

3. Look up the following verses and write the reality of this peace spoken of in each one.
    *   Numbers 6:26

    *   Psalm 29:11

    *   Isaiah 9:6-7

    *   Isaiah 52:7

- Isaiah 54:13

- Isaiah 57:19

4. How can you personally, practically apply what you have learned from your study of peace so far?

Peace is defined by an inner calm and spiritual well-being from God our Father and from the Lord Jesus Christ.

Would you say this characterizes your life?

1. Take the time to look up these last few verses that highlight peace. Write out the lessons you glean from each one and then spend time praying over each verse.

   • Ezekiel 37:36

   • Haggai 2:9

   • Acts 10:36

   • Romans 1:7

   • Romans 5:1

   • Romans 14:17

2. God's peace ('**shalom**') is a covenantal benefit of our relationship with Him through salvation in Jesus Christ. After spending a week on the spiritual fruit of peace, what are some practical ways you can cultivate the peace that comes from your relationship with the Lord? For example: some opposite actions that disrupt peace could be worry, complaining, or unbelief in the promises of God. What actions can you take in your life to combat the disrupters to peace?

3. Try this bonus activity: Find an empty box or jar in your home and label it: *For Jesus to do.* Determine that you will exchange any worry or disruption to your peace, write it down, and give it to Jesus. Place these things in the box and leave it in a place where you can see it often as a reminder to "*cast all your care onto Him, for He cares for you.*"

Week Five

The fruit of the Spirit is
Patience, Kindness, Goodness

We have spent the bulk of our study on the first three fruits or characteristics listed in Galatians 5:22: *love, joy, and peace.* Each of these qualities express the *Godward* aspect of the Christian life.

The fruit expressed this week reveals the *manward* aspect of our walk with the Lord. The fruit of the Spirit: *patience, kindness, and goodness* describe the way we relate to our fellow humans.

Patience, also called long-suffering, means courageous endurance without quitting. Kindness can also mean gentleness, and goodness is love in action.

1. The word patience, or long-suffering, is from the Greek word **makrothumia**. This is a compound word of **makros** which means long, and **thumos** which means anger or a strong, swelling emotion about something. When put together, **makrothumia** reveals the patient restraint of anger, or long-suffering, forbearance, or patience. How does knowing this Greek definition of patience further equip you to deal with each day or person in a patient way? Have you ever prayed for patience? In what ways do you need to become more adaptable to the people around you?

2. Read and write out Paul's command to us in Colossians 3:12.

3. Did you notice how Paul begins this verse by telling us to *'put on…patience'*? Explain how we are to do that as we are in Christ.

4. The Amplified version of Colossians 3:12 tells us that *patience is the power to endure whatever injustice or unpleasantness comes with good temper.* Keeping this definition in mind, look up the following verses on patience and write what you learn from each:

- Colossians 1:11

- Romans 2:4

- 1 Timothy 1:16

- 2 Peter 3:15

5. End this day in prayer over the things you have studied so far.

The first century believers faced unrelenting persecution. Every day they were confronted by hostile powers that were set against them, putting constant pressure on them to reject their faith and to return to their old ways.

James wrote to believers who were undergoing these hardships:

> *"Consider it nothing but joy, my brothers and sisters, whenever you fall into various trials. Be assured that the testing of your faith through experience produces endurance (patience) leading to spiritual maturity, and inner peace. And let endurance (patience) have its perfect result, and do a thorough work, so that you may be perfect and completely developed in your faith, lacking in nothing"*
> (James 1: 2-4 Amplified).

1. The word *'endurance'* is an accurate rendering of the word patience. It refers to staying power, holding on, perseverance, and never giving up. How does the writing of James in this passage encourage you? What is the biggest difficulty or pressure you are facing in your life right now, and how can this passage further equip you?

2. Have you had a time of needing the Lord to grant you endurance or patience during a previous trial or hard time? How did you see the Lord provide for you during that time? What did you learn from this time? How can you pass on what you have learned to someone else who may be enduring a trial?

3. Write out these two verses and tell what you learn about patience (*endurance*) from each one:

   • Revelation 1:9

   • 2 Thessalonians 3:5

4. Based on your study, write a working definition of patience.

Kindness is tender concern for others, reflected in a desire to treat people the way Jesus does. Kindness is deeply rooted in tender-heartedness and forgiveness. Kindness includes empathy, compassion, grace, and understanding.

1. Look up the following Scriptures and write out how kindness is portrayed in each one:

    *   Matthew 11:28-29

    *   Matthew 19:13-14

    *   2 Timothy 2:24

2. Write out Psalm 145:17 and explain how you have seen this to be true of the Lord in your own life.

3. Ephesians 4:32 reveals a practical way we are to live in kindness as evidenced by forgiveness. Re-write the truth of this verse in the form of a prayer.

4. Read Matthew 18:21-35 and summarize the graphic truth of this passage as it illustrates forgiveness and how we are to live it in our relationships with others. How does this passage strike you when you think of your own forgiveness from the Lord and the way you practice forgiving others? How does this brief study on kindness impact your relationships with others?

Our journey this week ends with the fruit of the Spirit of goodness.

We first hear the word goodness in Genesis 1:3 when God looked at what He created and declared it was good. The entire Bible cannot be exhausted when we dive into the Lord's goodness. His goodness is everywhere we look. In Exodus 33, we see how the Lord reveals His goodness to Moses with His presence.

Today's study on goodness barely scratches the surface, but we will look at a few verses that highlights the goodness of God and will end with a personal testimony—mine and yours!

1. Look up and write out each verse, then take the time to practice and declare exactly what each verse says:

    • 1 Chronicles 16:34

    • Psalm 23:6

    • Psalm 34:8

    • Psalm 107:1-2

    • Psalm 139:5

    • Psalm 143:5

2. How do you share the goodness of God with others, and especially with those who don't deserve it?

3. How do you experience the goodness of God?

4. What are some ways you intentionally cultivate an attitude of goodness to others? Use Micah 6:8 to answer.

This was not on my vision board!

On April 20, 2024, I arrived a few hours before our final Spring Flourish event would be happening. Many weeks of planning and preparation had gone into our luncheon for 250 women. We planned to gather in community, worship the Lord together, hear the stories of two new books being released, and focus on the personal importance of being in the Word of God each day.

I had many things on my to-do list before the doors opened, and so, to provide comfort as I walked around the church to do the many things, I decided on flip-flops for the win!

I was so busy and preoccupied doing the myriads of things (while comfortable in my flip-flops), I missed a step and took quite a tumble and landed on the floor.

I could tell immediately that the fall was a hard one, but I thought if I just recovered on the floor for a few minutes, I would be okay. I was wrong! To make a very long story short, I ended up having a terrible three-way break in my ankle requiring surgery and a hospital stay.

This was my first broken bone ever! I came out of surgery with a huge cast and strict directions not to put any weight on it for weeks.

Needless to say, this unexpected surgery and recovery radically changed my life. In fact, the entire ordeal canceled my life for about twelve weeks. Things I had planned, trips I had booked.... all were canceled and taken off my to-do list.

As soon as I began to realize the seriousness of my injury, I sensed the Holy Spirit reminding me that my response to this unplanned event would be everything. The precious Holy Spirit used this incident to cause me to reflect on the *goodness* of God amid hardship and injury.

The enemy's primary goal is to separate man from God. He will use anything to do this.

If I were to allow my injury to put distance in my relationship with the Lord, I would be on the losing end of everything.

My life was absolutely canceled for weeks, but Jesus met me at every turn and He showed me that God is bigger than a broken ankle! I learned that if I didn't fight Him regarding what had happened to me, but rather, surrender to Him in the midst, He would provide a peace and a joy I had never known.

No, this wasn't on my vision board, but I realized the Lord is still good even with a canceled life, a huge cast, daily discomfort, and weeks of not walking.

His goodness is revealed in His Presence and that is how I coped through twelve weeks of being sedentary. God is good.

Susie Larson, author of *Waking up to the Goodness of God,* writes:

> "God wants to move us out of bracing for impact and into a lifestyle of anticipating His goodness. He wants us to live with holy expectancy and believe He is always up to something good. Whether we perceive it or not, God is in the process of redeeming our story."

Week Five
Day Five

Use this day to write your own testimony of how God is redeeming your story. Prayerfully reflect on a time in your life (either past or present) where you counted on the ***goodness*** of God to help you through a difficult or unplanned situation.

Incluce in your story specifics of the Lord's **goodness** to you and to others. Also be sure to include the things you learned from this time in your life.

How are you living with holy expectancy and believing God is always up to something good?

As you wrap up this day and this week of study, take the time to review the previous four weeks. Go back and visit the JOY page and declare your praises out loud.

I highly recommend you read Susie Larson's book, *Waking up to the Goodness of God.* It is designed to be a 40-day journal of sorts, but it is so good, I read it straight through in one sitting! It impacted me so much, and little did I know, as I read it through a second time (slowly this time!), God was preparing me for what was to come. I was in the 'school' of His goodness, soaking Him up as I navigated Susie's book. It would be soon after reading her book for the second time that I would take that tumble and be sitting for many weeks.

Susie recommends we all declare out loud:

God is good.
I am loved.
Life springs up.
And I will flourish.

Week Six

The fruit of the Spirit is Faithfulness,
Gentleness, and Self-control

Week Six
Day One

This week we wrap up our study by looking at the final three fruits of the Spirit:

> *"But the fruit of the Spirit is love, joy, peace, patience, kindness, goodness, faithfulness, gentleness, self-control"* (Galatians 5:22).

The first three fruits revealed the Godward aspects of our walk with the Lord, and the next three fruits reflected the manward nature of our walk with God, or how we treat others. These final three qualities are more of an inward focus of our keeping in step with the Spirit, revealed in walking with Him each day. These final three fruits highlight what is going on inside of us.

1. Write out your definition of faithfulness here.

2. Look up the following Scriptures and write out the highlights of each one:

    *   2 Timothy 2:13

    *   Hebrews 11:11

    *   Hebrews 13:8

    *   1 John 1:9

    *   1 Corinthians 10:13

    *   1 Thessalonians 5:23-24

    *   Philippians 1:6

3. Based on your investigation of the verses above, write out a biblical definition of faithfulness.

4. Prayerfully read aloud Psalm 34 and write out a prayer of gratitude for the Lord's faithful love and presence in your life.

Read the true story of what happened to a missionary family in Haiti. This is written by my friend, Taran Long, and he has given me permission to share it with you.

I feel strongly that his story reveals God's faithfulness and His faithful fruit of the Spirit in the lives of His people.

After reading it, write out your thoughts and applications of the fruit of the Spirit of faithfulness.

Haiti Gang and God's Hand

My family and I moved to Haiti in 2001 some eight months after a short-term mission trip. We moved to that nation with the intention of helping to run other short-term mission teams. At that time, teams of twenty to sixty people would visit Haiti every other week to serve and assist with the work.

Within the first few months of living in Haiti, it came to the attention of the leadership that the school superintendent was corrupt. He was charging children to attend for his own profit, giving priority to family members, extorting money from directors and beyond. Steps needed to be taken.

The initial idea was to form a committee to oversee the schools versus having a single superintendent. The existing superintendent would be invited to be part of this new oversight committee, along with my father and several others. When he was confronted and this concept was introduced, he wanted nothing to do with it. The organization, therefore, decided to put my father in charge of the schools at this time, scrapping the idea of a committee. In short order, my dad began to take on more and more responsibility. Little did we know, this would start a multi-year battle with the disgraced leader.

His first move was to padlock and claim control of one of the schools. I remember going with my father to deal with this. When we arrived, we discovered that every classroom had been locked. My dad— utilizing a bolt cutter—reopened each of the classes. The school director and teachers were too scared to take such an action themselves. Thus, a parent-meeting was called to assure the Haitians that our organization would not yield to the pressures of this former leader.

In the days that followed, intimidation tactics were employed to cause us to quit (and leave Haiti). It started small. In the beginning, we had rocks thrown at us children as we played in the yard. Others would stop us on the road to frighten us. Several times I was pulled aside as a young boy by a Haitian teen or adult who sought to frighten me. Things worsened as one night the water supply to our campus was cut. Shortly thereafter, someone came in the middle of the night to set our generator on fire (causing us to live with minimal power for nearly six months). It became clear after a year or so that this man had formed a gang to get us to leave Haiti. If they could not get us to leave, they would work to destroy the mission.

The day after Christmas, two armed men came into our house and held family members at gunpoint in the middle of the night. I recall them waking up my parents. Dad kept trying to tell them we had no money on-hand (as it was secured at another building). My sister had a gun held to her head. Ultimately, the men had not come to harm us. Rather, they were trying to demonstrate how far they were willing to go to get us to leave and/or destroy the work of the Lord. In the end they stole a few items—including the new bikes we received for the holiday—and moved on. We learned after-the-fact that they secured access to our home after drugging the guards.

Such activities continued. The gang blocked the road out of campus with burning tires so that we could not leave. My father also had a cup of urine thrown on him. It was at this point that we sought police and judicial assistance. Restraining orders were filed on anyone we knew to be involved with the group. In a spirit of Christian outreach my father personally met with each of their families, wanting to make it clear that it was not our desire to see anyone imprisoned. Few things in life are as hellish as a Haitian prison! In the days that followed we also hired two undercover officers to travel with us.

Close to the end of that week, two gang members showed up on campus and stood in our yard with their arms crossed. Why? They were making it quite clear that we would have to arrest them, as they were not going to leave of their own volition. A whirlwind of events followed in rapid succession. My father, Roland and one of the other full-time missionaries got in our pickup and went to arrest the men. In Haiti, the police do not come to make arrest: you have to handle the situation! One of the gang members was taken into custody whereas the other escaped. My dad and his team made chase while I stayed with the team.

An hour later one of our workers came and found me in a panic. He told me that this whole event was a setup. Specifically, when my father and the others came back, the gang was waiting to stop them on the road and kill them. Once they were killed, the gang was purposing to come and kill those on the compound as well (i.e., including a short-term team we were hosting)! I quickly got the team into a secured location and told them to pray. I also picked the biggest man on the team and told him to follow me.

I tried everything I could to contact my father. However, in the frenzy of the arrest and chase, he had forgotten his phone. There was no way to reach him. All we could do at that moment was prepare for an attack. I remember meeting with our small security team, distributing whatever poles and machetes we had in our depot. We also piled rocks inside the chain-link fence in case we could not stop the assailants at the gate. As far as I knew, dad was already dead—and we would be dead soon as well.

Across town, my father dropped off the gang member at the jail and made way to come back to campus. Suddenly, they were stopped by someone running out of the sugar cane who warned them not to come back to campus! Thus, they returned to the police station and explained the situation to the officer. After some time spent convincing the local police to engage, my father and his group made way to the campus with a police escort—ready for a firefight.

Meanwhile, I was waiting for a fight for our lives back on campus. I do not remember telling my mom or sisters much. In the darkness of the night, we could see two small armies of people coming down the two roads that led to campus. My first thought was, "This is it...it's over." As they approached, my peers and I realized it was not the gang at all. It was two of the local villages! Hundreds of people showed up armed with fishing poles, rocks and machetes to defend us. They surrounded the campus and were prepared to make a stand with us. Another local village had also heard of this planned attack. They met with this gang on the road where they were waiting for my father and chased them away. In the end, my father and his team made it back safely (to my great relief).

After this event, my father sent my mother, my sisters and me out of the country for a time. He remained in Haiti to do everything possible to save the mission, as thousands of children and their families relied upon God's work in and through us. He went on national radio, coordinated marches with all of the villages and more to show the strength of the combined parents and families of our school children. In fact, one march through the village had nearly ten-thousand people! In time, certain members of the president of Haiti's secret service became involved. Within a month or so, several leaders of the gang had been arrested and others went into hiding. Dad ended up working with several groups to get two of the leaders moved to the penitentiary in Port-au-Prince.

Dad secured our home with additional security fencing around the yard. He also got a security dog (who turned out to be a great family pet as well). We all returned to Haiti and resumed the work of the Lord.

Things were quiet for about six months, though we had contingency plans if the violence resumed. My father also began to visit the imprisoned gang-leaders during this time. He would bring them food (you do not get food in Haitian prisons unless someone brings it to you) and try to positively connect with them.

In 2004 Haiti went through a civil war. The old military was reforming itself after having been disbanded by the President. This President was a wicked man, and many sought to overthrow him. Military forces formed in the north and in the southeast. In time, they marched to the capital. During this march they traveled through an array of cities, and at each one they would release the prisoners before burning the police station and jail (making them part of the growing army). When they arrived in the capital city of Port-au-Prince, they released all of the prisoners—including the two gang leaders my father had put there.

Shortly thereafter, we received word that the gang leaders were back in the village. Rumor was they planned to cut off our heads and burn our house. Most of the missionaries in the country had already pulled out or were in the process of leaving due to the deteriorating condition of the nation. It was becoming more dangerous by the day. We had friends who lived on a houseboat—friends who offered to remove us from the country and from the circumstance we found ourselves in. Yet, we had prayerfully determined that the safest place to be was in the center of God's will. We were called to Haiti and we knew that abandoning His work would mean abandoning the pastors, school directors and children we were meant to serve. Therefore, we chose to stay.

Through the morning I remember filling large barrels with water and placing them around the house in case of fire. Dad and I reviewed our escape plan and meet-up spots. Once again, I felt like this might be the end for us. Time passed and nothing happened. Evening came and, again, nothing happened. Later that night a message was sent to my father saying, "We want to meet with you tomorrow. We do not want to continue this, and we want to seek forgiveness."

The next day almost all of the members of the gang met with my father at his office. One-by-one they met with him, signing full confessions about their involvement and asking his pardon. They made commitments to never let something like this happen again. There were only two men who did not show up (i.e., one of them being the fallen superintendent who started this year-long scenario). As far as we knew he was still in hiding. Yet God had clearly done a great thing!

One month later, my father and I were driving home with two visitors who had come to spend time with our family. The original gang leader stopped us on the road. Like so many others, he asked for forgiveness and for my dad to pray with him. I took a picture of the two of them praying. I found it recently (see below).

This experience reveals much of the greatness and grace of God. Even in the midst of trials, the Lord cares about those whom we might deem as "enemies." Yet the Lord wants to bring about restoration! We need only continue doing what He has called us to do, letting Him take care of the rest.

Gentleness has been called bridled strength. Gentleness is the overflow of our lives when we keep in step with the Spirit. Like a garden, the soil must be tended to, and then healthy fruit appears.

Gentleness is meekness; it is not weakness or passivity; it is strength under control. What does this look like publicly? How is gentleness reflected when someone we know makes a mistake and it greatly affects us? How is gentleness reflected in giving someone the benefit of the doubt? What about when someone you're planning to see is late for your meeting? What about when something is lost or broken by someone else? How does gentleness come to play in these instances?

1. When the prophet Elijah was overwhelmed, disillusioned and disappointed, he ran off and was fearful. Read his story in 1 Kings 19:1-12. How did the Lord choose to speak to Elijah? Can you relate to Elijah's emotional response? How have you heard the gentle whisper of the Lord?

2. Write out the very practical instructions from 1 Peter 3:15. What additional things do you learn about gentleness in this verse?

3. What did Jesus have to say about gentleness in Matthew 11:28-30?

4. Complete today's lesson by finding another Scripture that teaches about gentleness. Write it out here and be prepared to share why you chose this verse.

Week Six
Day Four

Fruit grows in a climate blessed with an abundance of the Spirit and the Word. To walk in the Spirit is to keep in step with the Spirit. This means we do not run ahead, nor do we lag behind as we follow the leadership of the Spirit.

This really shows up when the conversation turns to the fruit of self-control as we seek to keep our spirit, soul, and body aligned with the Father, Son, and Holy Spirit.

1. Look up the following Scriptures that reflect the fruit of self-control. Write what you learn from each one and then summarize a working, biblical definition of self-control:

   • Romans 8:5

   • Proverbs 25:28

   • 2 Timothy 1:7

   • 2 Peter 1:5-7

   • Proverbs 29:11

   • Hebrews 12:1-3

   • Proverbs 16:32

   • 1 Corinthians 9:25-27

   • Summarize your findings in a biblical working definition of self-control:

2. As you read Titus 2:11-14, you will see how Paul condensed the saving plan of God into three realities: salvation from the penalty, power, and presence of sin. Take time to prayerfully read and study each verse and write what you learn from each one and relate it to the fruit of self-control.

_____

3. What encouraged you from your study of the Word today?

We end our final day of this study with a look at Jesus Himself.

Read Matthew 4:1-11. Read this passage several times and in several versions to get a strong feel for how Jesus demonstrated self-control to us.

1. Write your findings here and be sure to include anything new that jumped out to you from this passage. Your study Bible will most likely include some cross-references so that you can study other passages that highlight the actions of Jesus.

2. What do you specifically learn from Jesus about the fruit of self-control?

Works Cited

The Amplified Bible, Grand Rapids, MI: Zondervan Bible, 1983. Print.

Change Your Life Daily Bible, Carole Stream, IL: Tyndale House Publishers, 2010. Print.

The MacArthur Study Bible, Thomas Nelson, 2021. English Standard Version. Print

Larson, Susie. *Waking up to the goodness of God.* Nashville, TN: Thomas Nelson Publishers. 2024. Print.

Omartian, Stormie. *The Prayer that changes everything.* Harvest House Publishers. 2004. Print.

Renner, Rick, *Sparkling Gems from the Greek.* Teach All Nations. 2003. Print.

Schaefer, Marjie. *Choose Joy, A journey through the book of Philippians.* Flourish Through the Word. 2017

Schaefer, Marjie. *Flourishing Friendships.* Flourish Through the Word. 2023.

Wiersbe, Warren. *The Wiersbe Bible Commentary.* Colorado Springs, CO: David C. Cook. 2007. Print.

About the Author

Marjie Schaefer was born in Georgia, raised in Texas and has spent the past four decades in Washington state. She and her husband, Steve, have been married for 37 years and have four grown children and two grandchildren.

Marjie describes herself as an everyday girl who loves Jesus and daily pursues a life with Him at the center of her activities and purposes.

She started leading and teaching Bible studies while a student at Washington State University and has continued to open her home and her life to anyone who wants more of the Word and more of Jesus. Her greatest passion is bringing the Word of God to life through practical application and visual tools. Women look forward to her personal touches while attending her studies, and they usually go home with tangible reminders of God's love for them.

Marjie started spending deliberate and daily time in the Word of God while she was a young girl at the encouragement of her godly mother. This has given her a foundation that has stood the test of time. She began writing her own Bible studies at the request of some friends who desired to study the Word during the summer months.

Marjie and her team currently lead the ministry, *Flourish Through the Word,* a 501c3 non-profit organization which is a community of women in the greater Seattle region committed to being equipped through God's Word. As a result of their time together in God's Word, women move out into their arenas of influence, shining their light for Jesus.

Please visit *www.flourishthroughtheword.com* to find out more about Bible studies available for you or your church, along with various upcoming events.

About the Illustrator

JODI THORSEN:

I grew up in a home of artists, anything from painting, wood carving, furniture making, quilt designing to home decor. At an early age I was taught to appreciate what is around me and not to miss details. When you look at clouds they are not just white but they have various hues of gray, blue, purple, orange, pink and/or yellow.

My creative bent was always food—creating new recipes, making cakes or presenting food in an artistic way. I had never even thought to try painting. On one of my visits with my parents I asked my dad if we could paint together. In those few hours he shared how to look for the light and shadows, mixing colors and try not to be perfect.

During Covid I decided to pull out a canvas and paintbrushes. I was really hesitant knowing I had no training and really had NO idea what I was doing. I began with a prayer first and then remembered the Holy Spirit teaches all things. So why not painting? Then the Lord reminded me that in Exodus 31:1-5, "The Lord said, I have chosen Bezalel from the tribe of Judah and have filled him with the Spirit of God with skill, ability and knowledge in all kinds of crafts to make artistic designs for work in gold, silver and bronze." So, by faith, I asked the Lord to fill me and teach how to paint. I relied on Him for every stroke of the brush, the mixing of colors and the subject matter. He was faithful time and again.

I love to be creative and often have a need to create...something. I tell people often, "We all have a need to be creative in one form or another because God is our Creator and we were made in His image."

When I paint, my time with the Lord is like a slow dance—move this way, stop, turn... It's a constant fellowship and communion with Jesus. Asking Him such things as, "How do I paint a pearl so it looks real?" Guidance in capturing the correct color and light, or, "How do I paint what my spiritual eyes see?"

My heart's desire is to paint life-giving paintings that bring Him glory and speak to His children. What is even more amazing is the Lord has given me scriptures for almost every painting I have done.

I feel my paintings are an extension of His heart and nature. In the movie Chariots of Fire, Eric Liddell, an Olympic athlete said, "I believe God made me for a purpose—but he also made me fast. And when I run, I feel His pleasure." I feel the same way when I paint. I feel pure joy and experience His pleasure and one-to-one fellowship. Psalm 16:1, "...in your presence is the fullness of joy."

Painting Descriptions

Cherries:

I love cherries, anything cherry. As soon as I put the brush down from painting, the words, "Double Portion" dropped into my mind. I knew it was the Holy Spirit speaking to me. The scripture the Lord gave me was in Isaiah 61. It's titled" The Year of the Lord's Favor." This happens to be one of my favorite chapters. Isaiah 61:7 says, "instead of their shame my people will receive a double portion, and instead of disgrace they will rejoice in their inheritance; and so, they will inherit a double portion in their land and everlasting joy will be theirs."

Peach:

For my love of the South and all my friends who live there. "The more men are absorbed in My presence, the more they will reflect My glory. Self-absorbed people reflect their own glory which can't be compared to the glory of God." Donna Rigney

In 2 Corinthians 3:18, "And we all, who with unveiled faces contemplate the Lord's glory, are being transformed into his image with ever increasing glory, which comes from the Lord, who is the Spirit."

Fig:

"He told them this parable; Look at the fig tree and all the trees. When they sprout eaves, you can see for yourselves and know summer is near. Even so, when you see these things happening, you know that the Kingdom of God is near" Luke 21:29-30. Come Lord Jesus!

Pear:

"Every branch in me that does not bear fruit, He takes away; and every branch that continues to bear fruit, He (repeatedly) prunes, so that it will bear more fruit (even richer and finer fruit)" John 15:2.

This verse can sting but it is also so encouraging. Have Your way Lord and prune away.